Sassy CONFIDENCE

Because let's face it, confidence will make you irresistible, and being sassy is just so much fun!

JASMINE BEAUSOLEIL

BALBOA
PRESS

A DIVISION OF HAY HOUSE

Interior Graphics/Art Credit: François L'Heureux

Balboa Press books may be ordered through booksellers or by contacting:

Balboa Press
A Division of Hay House
1663 Liberty Drive
Bloomington, IN 47403
www.balboapress.com
1 (877) 407-4847

Print information available on the last page.

ISBN: 978-1-5043-3090-9 (sc)
ISBN: 978-1-5043-3091-6 (e)

Balboa Press rev. date: 5/26/2015

Contents

Acknowledgements

A book is never created by only one person, trust me, I know! Several people come together, whether they are aware of it or not, to help create the end product.

Let me first thank the Universe for giving me the opportunity to live another incarnation on our beautiful planet with all that it entails; the good and the "oh what the hell?!" moments, hahaha!

I want to thank my husband, Donald Doherty, who supports me in his own way even if it's not always obvious to me, I've come to understand that without him, much of all I've accomplished would have taken a different turn. Thank you for your patience and your support.

A special thanks to my parents who were able to navigate the murky waters of their lives to bring us (my sisters and I), all we needed to live healthy, often by depriving themselves. My heart and soul are filled with these generous gifts you have given and all the lessons you taught me.

To my older sister, thank you. Early on in life you fought for what you believed in and it gave me the courage to do the same.

Thank you to my little sister who embodies sensitivity ... how I would like to help you with these lines!

A great big thank you to all my friends, past and present, who have helped in many ways; through our conversations, exchanges and your simple presence. Last but not least, thank you to my clients who have showed me again and again that what I give comes back to me many times over.

Every single person mentioned here, and even those who are not for the sake of trying to keep things short and sweet; you are all a big part of my life and you all hold a special place in my heart.

THE SECRET OF MAKING DREAMS COME TRUE CAN BE SUMMARIZED IN FOUR C'S.
THEY ARE CURIOSITY, CONFIDENCE, COURAGE, AND CONSTANCY;
AND THE GREATEST OF THESE IS CONFIDENCE.

- WALT DISNEY

Introduction

Imagine this: you, yes you; you're sitting there looking cute in that new outfit you just bought and feeling pretty good, hoping that someone will notice you. Then *she* walks in. Just one glance and you are jealous and at the same time in admiration. She seems to have it all; the walk that makes her look like she is gliding across the room, the smile on her lips and the light in her eyes that would make even the biggest glacier melt. Confidence just oozes out of her every pore and you know, nothing can stop this woman and no one can resist her. All of a sudden you don't feel so cute anymore and you have this sinking feeling that you pale in comparison and the urge to go home starts to creep up on you.

Sounds familiar? Has this or a similar situation, ever happen to you? Have you ever caught yourself thinking "That woman is really strong and confident; I wish I was like that"?

Well, you are not alone my friend, millions of women feel like that. After all, early on we are taught to be good, nice little girls. Later, we are taught to be good hard workers or stay at home moms, to be there for our families, to cook, clean, take the kids to the soccer game, have diner ready when our husband comes home, etc. But who teaches us how to be courageous, confident and passionate women? Up until now, no one! You were on your own, but no more. This book contains everything you should have been taught to let your sassy confidence shine all over your world!

So, are you ready?

Let's get started!

What it is and what it's not

S adly, I have come across women who are almost scared to be confident because they confused confidence, with arrogance. So, before we get ahead of ourselves here, I want to make sure that we are really clear on what being confident really is so that we don't mistake it for anything else.

First, confidence is not arrogance. Arrogance is thinking and acting like you are better, smarter and more important than others which makes you presumptuous, overbearing and probably insulting too. Confidence, on the other hand is a feeling, or rather I should say the consciousness of one's own power in any and every circumstance; it is believing that you can act in a right, proper, effective way in order to succeed in anything you put your mind to. It is a state of powerful yet quiet inner certainty that gives you the tools to go where you want and get what you want while regarding others as your equals, because you know that they are as valuable as you are.

Confidence has nothing to do with religious upbringing, ethnicity, education and even less of your weight or appearance. It won't come around when you lose 10 pounds, get that fancy diploma, get your nose fixed or get that promotion you want. As a matter of fact, it's the other way around; confidence is what will get you all of those things, (ok, not the nose job but you won't need it anyway!). And believe it or not, it won't come from people accepting or praising you. Again, it's rather the other way around: people will accept and praise you once you have gained that which they seek for themselves: confidence.

1

You see, people look up to those who have confidence because confidence is strength and power – ie: survival. In Paleolithic times, we were wired to seek and align with those who had the most chance for survival. That meant to look for people who were healthy and strong. Today, survival equals success, so unconsciously we are attracted and want to copy those who look and feel successful, ie: confident. Before you reach such a state of being, you are but a drop of water in the ocean, mirroring and merging with all the other drops.

What you need to realize is that; that drop of water, is very powerful. Yes, in the grand scheme of things, we are just one measly drop amongst many others. But you must come to understand the power of that drop; first, imagine if you were in the desert, how precious that drop would be to you or any living being for that matter. Water is impressive, one drop is as impressive as the millions of others put together, it possesses the same qualities you do; it can change form with the seasons, it creates, sustains and save lives. But it can also erode and change its environment with a force that nothing can resist, gushing from everywhere or slowly and patiently carving its way. It can be tamed and/or used to power machines and produce electricity etc. Women do this too; we all have those unique qualities (well maybe not produce electricity or power machines), but I'd rather be either spilling over or slowly carving my way on the world and changing it, then to be tamed. What about you?

After all; water makes up 70% of our bodies, 70% of our planet and 90% of all plant life.

But this drop is very powerful, as the following article describes, written in this 1928 article entitled: The power of a drop of water from The Children's Treasure house.

Water is very powerful and we are made of about 70% of water. Imagine all those drops working with you towards being more confident. That's the power that you hold!!

Water needs no one to tell it what to do and how to do it, it just does what it does best, that is to be strong. So go ahead, tap into that power add it to the knowledge you will find here and let your sassy confidence come out and shine!

Wait! One more thing… Let's look at the definitions I found for the word Sassy:

The Urban dictionary's definition is:

Possessing the attitude of someone endowed with an ungodly amount of cool.

Another's definition goes like this:

Fun, daring, sexy, and multifaceted and boldly smart someone you have to have.

Then there is always a low-down-bummer that I will share with you just because it exists and I don't want you to think I withheld the information from you, this other definition states that a sassy person is insolent and impertinent. Honestly, this last definition sounds more like arrogance to me, but hey, there you have it: the cake, the icing and an annoying piece of egg shell in your first bite. LOL

The reason behind this book

Since there is a reason for everything, there is of course a reason for me to be sitting here typing away tirelessly at my keyboard to bring you this work of love. Well, there are actually two reasons...

First - I struggled for many years with confidence issues because of my upbringing (or so I thought). My parents did the best they could and I love them so very much, but since no child comes with a "how to" guide, they made do with what they knew; their own insecurities, fears and financial situation. As a little girl, I can still remember the hardship that my parents went through: the company that my dad worked for went on lock out and dad found himself jobless when my sisters and I were very young. My mother was an auxiliary nurse on call at a hospital and didn't get called very often. Thank God we lived on a farm and the animals fed us for a while but as with all animals, you have to care for them too. It got to a point where my parents had to ask for charity to put food on the table. Few people really know what it means to be hungry but we sure did! When you sit outside and look at the cows eating grass and think "hey, maybe I can eat that too." Trust me; you've been hungry for a while! Of course as life goes, things tend to get worse before they get better... the house my parents rented caught on fire. My parents braved the flames to salvage whatever they could and we were tossed from one family member's house to another until a few months later we were able to move back into our smoke-scented-not-so-finished rented house.

After this episode, my parents were pretty desperate and tensions ran high in the house. Already, it wasn't always a peaceful place, but with this much burden on their shoulders, patience was utterly inexistent. After trying many different approaches to their financial situations and seeing all the could-be-solutions fail, I remember my father sitting at the kitchen table one night trying to draw up a plan to rob a bank. Yes you heard me. He would go to jail to feed his family; now that is some fatherly love right there! Anyway, the Universe flows in such a way that his plan didn't need to come to past, he got offered a job (correctional service officer – so he did go to jail, just not on "that" side of the bars)... He was posted on the other side of the continent. For months on end, we lived without a father until we got moved to join him. No one but my father spoke English then, being right in the middle of the school year when we got moved we needed to learn fast. New province, new friends, new house, new language, I loved it but it wasn't all peachy for everyone and getting accepted by our peers wasn't a piece of cake either.

Anyway, we settle into our new home, new routine and learned the language, and then my mother got really sick. At first, they didn't know what was going on; it took a few months to figure out that it was Multiple Sclerosis. We were just kids; my oldest sister was 10, I was 8 and our younger sister was only 5. My father was the sole income of the family as my mother lay in a hospital bed for 6 months, completely paralysed from the arm pits down; as the doctors tried to figure out what she had (the disease wasn't really well known then) and started the treatments.

My father couldn't stop working to stay by his beloved wife; he had to provide for all of us with the very stressful job that, to this day, I still don't know how he managed to stay there all those years without losing his mind or his humanity. He was a medium to maximum correction officer. He has seen and been through some pretty horrible stuff and it had repercussions. When you see such "un-humanlike" humans, you are always on the defensive, ready for an attack and you fear for the lives of your loved ones; so he was really, really strict about everything: how we dressed, our school grades, our friends (or lack thereof). I guess his past emotional pains combined with his job created the perfect cocktail to develop anger management issues. So compliments were few and far between, instead we were scorned for many, many things. Confidence didn't have its place as standing up for your self was seen as an act of defiance.

Listen, I'm not going to tell you all the details of that sob story and I'm not telling you this so we can all have a cry fest, but rather to paint you a picture of my background and how far I have come so you know that you can do the same!

By the way, for those who are wondering; I **don't** have any Mommy or Daddy issues. I know in my heart that I chose them as parents to walk this path with me so I could teach others that yes; your past does shape you, but it doesn't have to drag you down. As a matter of fact, if you so choose, it can lift you up far beyond what you expected. But we'll get back to this a little later.

Second – It is my opinion (and I know I'm not the only one that thinks like this) that women are more powerful than they even dare to dream. And therein lies the problem; they don't dare enough to see, even less use, all this power vested in them. But I see it in all the women I coached; that deep hidden "want" to be a confident, sassy, sexy, delightful risk-taking-courage-roaring woman. And you know what, **you can**! But I'll do better than just tell you that you can; if anyone tries to tell you that you can't, give them my information, I'll gladly tell them off – *kindly* - for you! *Wink*

So there you have it, my two reasons that keep me digging for answers, so I can bring you tips and tricks that if applied can bring out your inner shine with all the magnificence that you are! I truly believe that our world would change for the better if women started to shine brighter; that's why I'm writing this "how to" guide and that's also why I created the "Sassy confidence" movement.

To find out more about the Sassy Confidence Movement
check out our Facebook page to find out what's
happening now at: www.fb.com/sassyconfidence
or follow us on twitter:
www.twitter.com/sassyconfidenc1

Also, you can have a look at our 30 days motivational deck of cards.
They are loaded with gorgeous pictures and of course, great quotes!
Take a look on Pinterest: http://www.pinterest.com/sassyconfidence/
Grab yours today!

Best kept secret

Before we go any further, there is a secret I want to share with you; it's a hidden piece of our history – the history of women. You see, I studied the feminine divine - a "religion" before that of patriarchy - a story well hidden, not to be taught in schools. This story takes place in the Neolithic Age; at the time when women were revered, especially those who had curves. They were above all, the most beautiful, sensual and they respected them. Because curves were a sign of health, prosperity and reproductive power of the woman in question. Her femininity lay in the generous curves of her body. The women were so respected at that time that the common belief was that God was actually a woman. Can you believe that! There was, of course, a male God, but it was her subordinate. The feminine aspect prevailed with peace, quiet and beauty for hundreds of years. It is only during the advent of patriarchy that men tried to silence the great power of women becoming, by force, her superior. They dethroned the Goddess who nourished the people and was the guardian of peace; male religion, psychologically and physically assaulted women to become the prevailing religion. Men declared a "war of religion" on the female ways declaring that all those who worshiped femininity and all that it represents were sent from the devil and would be severely punished. No need to dwell on the subject, everyone knows the horrifying stories of witch hunts, but these horrors begun long before that time. Anyway, this is what the accumulation of archaeological evidence of Neolithic age tells us.

These horror stories are all over the history that we teach our children and then we wonder why women have such low self-esteem and confidence…

For a long time, women were seen as only that which has in it the ability to conceive children. In other words, a thing – that gives birth. Historically, women were considered not only inferior to men, but also as a source of temptation and vile. For example, in Greek mythology it is a woman (Pandora), who opened the forbidden box that brings disease and despair to humanity. Roman premises described women as well as children; forever inferior to man.

In Christian theology, these perceptions were perpetuated. St. Jerome, a Latin priest 4th century Christian church said: "Woman is the gate of evil and the passage of malice, the bite of the serpent, in a word, it is a dangerous object." Thomas Aquinas, a Christian theologian of the 13th century said: "The woman was created to be the servant of man, her only role is conception ... since for other tasks humans would be better assisted by other men."

The myth of the natural inferiority of women greatly influenced the status of women in relation to the law. In England, a married woman was defined as one with her husband; she left her name and almost everything she had found under the tutelage of her husband.

Early in the history of the United States, a man literally had his wife and children. They were the equal of any other object of his possession. If a poor man decided to send his children to the poor house, the mother was helpless and did not have any say in the matter. Some communities had changed the law so that a woman can own certain property but only with the permission of her husband.

In the early nineteenth century, it was considered disrespectful for a woman to speak before an assembly.

Thank goodness since then, the world has changed and it can still change. Our perception of women is distorted. It's time to take control and realize the greatness and beauty of real women, by taking control of our own bodies and our own lives.

Side note: Don't be mistaken, this is not a book from or for the feminist movement. I actually believe that the feminist movement was a bit extreme in its goal for equality. A woman must be a woman and act like a woman, whatever that means for you. Should she be underestimated? NO! Should she be underpaid? HELL NO! But we as women can't, in all honesty, think that we can do *everything* that a man does and men can't do *everything* that women can. That's just the way things are: I mean really, we don't even think alike so stop being like a guy and be a woman already!

However, to achieve this humble goal, we must go beyond the vision of that religion and society has imposed upon us… one that we have blindly accepted for too long.

« *The World will be saved by the western woman.* »

~ Dalai Lama

… so you see, I was right, I'm not the only one who thinks women are powerful, the Dalai Lama thinks so too! ☺

But in order to resonate with this, you must first learn to love yourself. Yes, I know, it's cliché but it's also true!

Here is a little mission, if you choose to accept, to get you started on that self-love road: look deep into your eyes in the morning – after you have washed and put your face on, otherwise you might scare yourself (just kidding!) actually doing this with no make-up is even better – and say : "I love you".

Say it like you really mean it, like if you were saying it to a child. Your inner little girl really needs this love from you. The first step to self-confidence is self-love.

With the following tips and tricks, you'll raise that sassy self-confidence of yours and you'll be on your way to change the world!

Know thy self

"If you are going through hell, keep going" - Winston Churchill

He had it right you know! If I were to be going through hell, I know that where I come from got me there so I wouldn't turn around and go back, and I sure wouldn't want to stay stuck in that situation. You can bet your pretty little butt that I'd keep moving! That's the thing though, some people whine about what they are going through but they just "stay there" because they think that whatever situation or problem they are in, it's not their fault. Well, to those people I say this: *"my dear, it is really sad to see you lose yourself like that, but your reaction is not very mature and not very enlightened."*

Please, don't be offended; I say this with the utmost respect and empathy. You see; I was there, I did that, 'till the day I decided I had enough. So I know how you feel but I also know things can change when we change what we do, how we think and how we react. Stop looking at the entire world/universe for answers to the infamous "why me?" question. Because:

The answer lies within.

I use to ask myself the same questions, I use to doubt myself every single day, I use to wonder if I was doing the right thing, I use to ask the universe for signs that would let me know if I was on the right path, I use to ask people their opinion of everything from how I looked in those jeans to their opinion on what I was doing, if they thought it was a good idea or not, etc. I use to wonder if people liked me and would often think they had better things to do or better people to hang out with then me, etc. Until I realized that if I felt good inside, it would be reflected on the outside and if I truly did my best i.e.: stop procrastinating and get stuff done, I would feel good inside. And when I felt good, people genuinely wanted to hang out with me, they called me up - not the other way around - totally a sign that they think highly of you!

Yeah, I am a firm believer that the Universe sends you signs... lots of them. If "shit is hitting the fan" so to speak, the Universe is telling you to turn the fan off! Go within, learn who you are, what you really like and concentrate on that.

What you give attention to is amplified
and
what you ignore disappears.

The first time I came across that line was in the 1998 movie *Merlin*. I can't remember if it was those exact words that Merlin used but its close enough for me. That quote stayed with me and **had a really big impact on my life**. I have been living by it and it has made my life sooooo much easier in every aspect!

So, to make a long story short, if you want more confidence, the first thing to do is look at yourself; what are you doing - or not doing - that keeps you stuck where you are? Confidence comes from knowing that you can. So start there: what CAN you do? Don't hesitate to write seemingly insignificant things because sometimes it's the "insignificant" stuff that can move mountains. Really spend some time with this question, you don't have to give me an answer and there is no time limit - except for the one you impose upon yourself. This is not a test and there are no wrong answers! Look at whatever situation you are in **right** now and ask yourself: what can I do to make this better? Can I act or think in a different way? Is there anything that I can do to raise my positivity levels so **that I can see solutions** that I'm missing because of a negative state of mind? (Honestly - if there is nothing else that you do, do this one!!)

Of course, if you know your abilities, your strengths and your limits, this may be easier to answer and to make a list of those things. They will be there for you to refer back to whenever you judge yourself too harshly. This may also help to raise your positivity levels.

For those wondering what a positivity level is here's a brief explanation:

Positive psychology teaches us that the neuropath ways in our brains are plastic, which means they can change and adapt. Humans where once chased (yep, way back when... we weren't so high on the food chain) so we developed an outlook on life that allows us to spot negative or harmful situations faster than we spot positive ones. Today, that which kept us safe, pretty much keeps us from moving forward in life, but it's not all bad. I mean, you have to have a certain amount of keep-your-eyes-peeled-for-threatening-situations engrained inside of you so that you don't go walking in a dark alley in a less then favorable neighborhood with an expensive purse hanging on your shoulder and expect that little trip to end well. There needs to be a balance between negative outlook and positive outlook. It's not supposed to be all sunshine but it's not supposed to be all dark either. We are "wired" to see the negative stuff first – its survival, so because of this, in the beginning it does require some effort to spot the positive and raise your positive levels so they are - eventually - equally as present as the negative ones.

To sum things up: you want to foresee the dangers ahead but you don't want them to keep you from moving forward! Positivity levels lets you see the danger AND the solutions to avoid it or deal with it if it can't be avoided. So you see, positive psychology isn't about seeing life with rosy glasses and making up fairy-tale fantasies about how things are, positive psychology is about bringing your mind to a point where you will see the negative stuff but it won't affect your happiness level because you will know that you can do something about it.

Ok so here are a few things you should really have in check, this will help you to raise your positivity levels and gain the self-confidence you want:

Do you get enough sleep?

This might sound far from subject but sleep plays a really big role on our perception of life. Studies - and personal observations/experience - show that when you are tired, your brain is more likely to stir-up darker thoughts and feelings. You'll criticize yourself and others more, you don't seem like you can do anything right, those infamous thought "why me" and "I'm not good enough" will pop up, etc. Not good for confidence!! Over the years I realized that I was more self-critical when I was tired. So now, when I hear "ego voice" talk trash about me or what I'm doing. I notice it and say to myself:" Oh ok. I know what's going on here, I'm just tired." and the negative self-talk immediately ceases. Just like magic! And then I go to bed earlier and know that I'll feel better in the morning.

Note: if you have a habit of being tired, check with your doctor to make sure it's not a medical condition (depression, sleep apnea, thyroid, etc.). Once that has been eliminated, check your evening activities. If you go to bed too late because you want to watch that late night show you are use too... it might be a good idea to tape it and watch it the next day. I encourage you to rethink your sleeping schedule. It will take you a couple of days to adjust to going to bed, and falling asleep earlier but in due time you'll get there and trust me, this is tremendously helpful and will make you feel more energetic.

Food and exercise are your friends

Now, I'm not a nutritionist or a kinesiologist but I am a naturotherapist so I know my share on the subject. I'm not going to dive into this too deep because I'm not writing a book on the subject, but I will tell you this: food and exercise play a big role in how you feel and the happier you are the more confident you'll be. So it wouldn't be fair for me to write a book on the subject of confidence without slipping a word or two in here on the matter.

Ok here's the big line: What you eat and the exercise you do influence your hormones. Endorphin, oxytocin, dopamine and serotonin are the "happy hormones" that our brain creates and sends to our body. They are highly sensitive to what we eat and our brain liberates them into our system during or after exercise. In other words; exercising and eating right doesn't only make you look good, it makes you feel good too. Ain't that a **great** bit of information right there!

I guess it won't come as a big surprise then, if I invite you to get the help you need to move towards better eating habits and moving your sexy booty more often! Right! Good ☺

Fiew! Glad that's over, right? Yeah, me too! But the difference between someone who has confidence/success (to me those two things are almost synonymous) and someone who has less (or none) of those things, is the actions they will take after getting a piece of information. So make sure you actually take action after each tips in this little book. Hey, you want more confidence; you want a better life and more success right?! I mean, that's why you got this book, isn't it? Do this for <u>yourself</u>, no one else will.

Intuition, your most potent tool

I've trusted the still, small voice of intuition my entire life.

And the only time I've made mistakes is when I didn't listen.

~ Oprah

C all it gut instincts if you want, call it the little voice or inspiration but whatever name you choose intuition will save you a world of hurt, mistakes and anguish. Intuition is my most potent self-confidence tool! You'll never fall for the wrong guy again or get the wrong job, or take the wrong road for that matter. Imagine; all those super-duper masters of self-help and personal development "gurus" you've been following, well... you'll be just like them!

Don't get me wrong, it takes courage to listen, to trust and to act upon that little voice inside, but once you've taken that chance - and done so a few times - you'll soon trust it and just like Oprah says, it pays off!

Intuition has been part of my life for as far as I can remember. When I was a child, nothing could convince me other than my own inner voice. I have to say that I was a highly "sensitive" child (you were probably one too because we were all sensitive – or should I say sentient beings, at some point). But later in my adolescent years, I discovered that not everyone was like that and, like every other teen, I wanted to fit in, so I shut it out, or rather pushed it down; quite like one would do with a balloon in a pool. That's when I started to feel insecure and unsure of pretty much everything; from the way I looked, to what I wanted to do with my life all the way down to my choice of friends. I let the noise of the world and the opinions of other people stir me away from my own inner voice, in other words; I gave them my power. Confidence is power people, don't forget it!

Anyway, after I went through the "I'm-creating-my-own-image-by-copying-everyone-else's" phase that all the teenagers have, I got tired of being someone else. I felt a yearning to become me again, but I had lost that person and sometimes when you lose something you can search a while before you find it again. So I started to "reclaim" my own identity. How? By daring to be me; daring to listen to that little voice inside and … (dramatic music paying)… following it! As scary as that was because it meant that maybe people wouldn't like me anymore because I wasn't "like them" anymore and worst yet, I wasn't the person they had come to know anymore. It's a slow process but it could have been faster had I had a group of women to help me along (like the Sassy Confidence movement… you know, *wink, wink).

I studied everything and anything on the subject of personal development. Seriously, you should see my shelves and my collection of certificates! It's too bad they don't teach you this in stuff in school or that parents don't know how to go about teaching their kids these things.

Well, after all those books, seminars, workshops, consultations and a few good years of experience, I realized one thing of GREAT value: No one knows better than me.

Let that sink in for a minute....

I'm not telling you this to be impudent. Let's face it, no one knows better than you either. You can go to school, read all the books become a psychologist if you want but not even the super qualifies knowledgeable people know you like you know yourself....even if you have lost yourself in others noisy opinions. This is where intuition comes in really handy.

You should weigh everything you see, hear or feel against your inner guidance; it will guide you to the truth, what is good, or not good for you and much more.

**Listening to your intuition will get you
almost every answer you seek.**

As Albert Einstein said:
*"The intellect has little to do on the road to discovery. There comes
a leap in consciousness, call it intuition or what you will, and the
solution comes to you and you don't know how or why."*

It's easy but not simple: all you have to do is listen. This is an art we have fallen behind on in our society but it is easy to do. Listen to your feelings – no, not your emotions, your feelings. How do you feel about "this person", is she or he a good person? Is this job good for you? Is this relationship healthy? Etc. The first feeling that comes up is often the good one. After that, the rational parts of our mind kick in and we question everything to its core.

The "feelings" or whispers of intuition are often very quiet and quick. If you don't pay attention enough to your inner voice, you'll miss it. So you have to practice listening. Here's a couple of ways to do this:

First, you have to be in the right state of mind: non-judging, quiet and open.

Then practice:

1) Whenever you meet a new person ask yourself how you feel in this person's presence – do you feel safe, do you feel as if they are honest, caring, etc.
2) Take a walk outside and try to "know" the color of the car coming up behind you before you see it.
3) When someone calls, "guess" who it is before you answer - this one works better at home than at the office ;)
4) Try it with food. Should I be eating this, if I want to stay healthy or lose weight, etc.? And sense the answer within. *Also listen for the feeling of satiety – another thing we have lost touch with.*
5) Practice with a friend and colored paper; try to guess which color they've picked, etc.

Your everyday decisions will become easier and easier once you've learned to trust your inner guidance and because of that inner self-trust, you'll be more confident. I promise.

Developing greatness

Alright, here's the thing: I'm convinced that every soul has greatness inside of them just begging to come out and be seen, heard or felt. The problem is that we barely scratch the surface of what we can do in one lifetime because most of us are either too scared to try step out of our comfort zone or too busy working for a living... so we have no time to live

I've always found this to be ridiculous; there are so many things to enjoy and we stop ourselves, sometimes even before we allow ourselves to dream – that's even before we let others stomp on those half dreamt dreams of ours. Then we let ourselves be dragged silently into the mould that society wants us to fit in – be it for your work, your appearance, who treats your ailments, and everything else. But a few years back, I was delighted to hear about a woman who dared to talk about a touchy subject: Bronnie Ware worked for a long time in palliative centers and wrote a book on the 5 things the dying regret the most. Here are those things:

- I wish I'd had the courage to live a life true to myself, not the life others expected of me.
- I wish I didn't work so hard.
- I wish I'd had the courage to express my feelings.
- I wish I had stayed in touch with my friends.
- I wish that I had let myself be happier.

Doesn't it make sense then, that to develop your own inner greatness you should do these things before you arrive at the end of your journey? YES! Totally and uncensored. And that, my friends, is why I'm writing this book. I want women to step up to be the leaders in the art of being courageously who they really are. I know we are experts at keeping everything inside so we don't disturb anyone, keep up good appearances, work hard, align with what everyone else is saying, etc. Men do it to of course, but this book is for my ladies out there so I'll concentrate my work on you. ☺

The more you listen to your inner guidance, the stronger and the more confident you'll get, but if you add to that the expression of your own soul, you become unstoppable!

Here's what I mean; women are creators! You knew that right? So create something that means something to you. Try new things. You never know what you'll fall in love with; it could be dancing, high wire walking, fine arts, embroidery, hair stylist, makeup artist, jewelry maker, cook, health or fitness, writing, accounting, firefighting, etc. Look, there's a gazillion things that you can try out there. Try one, than another until you find something that clicks; something that makes your heart sing and then, become excellent at it. That, my friend, is an excellent way to pick up some major confidence points! Sometimes, people stop and settle for less because they tried a lot of things and still haven't found what pleases them. I know a thing or two about that! But I tried to settle; it didn't feel good, I actually felt like I was going to plunge into a deep depression. So I put aside what everyone else thought and even my own fears and doubts, I pulled my sleeves up and decided to push through. And you know what; it was well worth all the trials. I absolutely LOVE what I do now!

So don't let fear get in your way. It's easy to feel afraid when you step out of your comfort zone. Feel the fear but do it anyway. After all, as Will Smith said so well in the movie After Earth: "Fear is not real. It is a product of thoughts that you create…" This, I have found to be true. Fear is a measurement that tells us how far we are from our comfort zone. Once you did something that you once feared, isn't it easier to do it again? If you repeat it 100times, wouldn't you feel less afraid?

> One more thing: don't let anyone, not even yourself, tell you that you can't be great at whatever you chose to be great at!

Oh and don't wait until whatever you decide to do is perfect before you talk about it or present it to the world because remember, amateurs built the ark. Professionals built the Titanic… Food for thought!

Caring do's and don'ts

T ake a look at the image below; the woman on the right is tall, thin beautiful, yet she seems to be worried about what the other woman is thinking about her. The other woman seems to care less and seems to feel totally at ease with herself. This is one example of many, but as you will see, it "sets the table", about this subject – so to speak.

Don't get me wrong, caring about others, animals and even things is a good thing, what am I saying: it's a very good thing. It's in our nature to care, even more so as women. We care about our friends and families wellbeing (yes that includes our pets and our plants). We want to help them out, mostly because helping others is a demonstration of our love and appreciation. Right? Totally! But sometimes we get caught up in a whirlwind of emotions and forget why we do what we do and what we are supposed to do with all that caring.

To build confidence, you have to be able to draw the line between when to care and when to pull the plug – so to speak. Because you see, caring the way that we do, is not always a good thing. Look, some of us have this tendency to put the wellbeing of others above our own. I was like that too, until I discovered that it doesn't help; not them and certainly not me. Sure, I felt good to have helped them; you get that flattering: "oh my gosh, thank you, you're such a good friend (or sister or daughter or girlfriend – pick one)" bit. But then, sometimes years later, you realize that this friend – or family member - is always in the same kind of predicament and always asking for help. That's when the feeling of "having" to help sets in, rather than "wanting" to help. It can go all the way to feeling like this person is taking advantage of your kindness... Sorry girl, this is never a good place to be in.

There's a saying that goes like this: "Give a man a fish and you feed him for a day. Teach a man to fish and you feed him for life."

So when someone asks you for a favor, think: will this serve this person in the long run? What's their history of asking for this kind of help? What are they really doing to help themselves in this situation? And finally, but not the least, is this going to impede on my wellbeing; be it physical, emotional, financial or time that I had for something else that is important to me?

What I'm saying is on the same lines as what they say on the videos when you take a plane: **put the oxygen mask on you first!** Then help the other person next to you, even if it's a child. After all, you can't help if your batteries aren't full! So consider these don'ts:

- If you're struggling for money, don't lend any
- If you barely have time to do what needs to be done in your own life, don't take time on your schedule to help someone else.
- If you're on a negativity diet and someone is complaining about their every problem, don't listen. Tell them to change the subject or do what you have to do to avoid them…nicely.

Also, on the don'ts list: Caring about what other people say about you or what they think you can or can't do. You are the master of your own life. Who are they to decide what you can or can't do? What did they do to make them experts on **your** abilities? My guess is; nothing! So why do you care about their opinion?

Most people resist change, they are scared to step out of their comfort zone. If you have a personality that is different or want to do something out of the ordinary, you'll meet a lot of naysayers. They are speaking out of their own fears or personal beliefs, how they were brought up to think etc. If you really want a good opinion – the type that really counts – find someone who has walked in your shoes and succeeded!

Here are some do's (can I really say that? Oh yes I can!):

- If you want to be more positive, hang out with positive people
- If you are self-conscious, hang out with people who are confident
- If you want to be successful, hang out with people who are already there
- If you want to lose weight, hang out with healthy, active people

Here's why: Neuroscience has discovered that there's a part of our brain that is used to mimic other people's emotions and behaviors. They are called the mirror neurons and we use them, without even knowing it, to learn new skills by copying others. All warm blooded creatures have these mirror neurons, this is how we learn to speak, copy facial expressions, emotional reactions and much more. Needless to say that this gives a whole new meaning to the quote by Jim Rohn that says : *"You are the average of the five people you spend the most time with."* This was Jim Rohn's belief and it's now a scientific fact. So, who do you hang out with?

Hey, if you're reading this book, my guess is that you want more confidence and thus a better life for yourself – come hang out with likeminded women at <u>www.fb.com/sassyconfidence</u>. We've walked in your shoes and can really support you to get the confidence your want! Also, follow us on twitter.com/Sassyconfidenc1

Body/mind connexion,
your secret weapon

Your body is the perfect tool. What you experience through your body will make your mind think it's real and vice versa.

Ok wrap your mind around this juicy life changing piece of information: your mind and your body are connected in ways that are more subtle than what science dares to share, or even to look into for that matter. But we know better, don't we?! I mean, you can't deny that when you feel down, you tend to make yourself smaller than when you feel really happy, right. And when you force yourself to smile of laugh when you're not feeling up to par, you'll feel better in now time. You can't be angry and smile at the same time and you can't feel unconfident when you take a confident pose. It's just the way it is.

This is nice and all, but like you, I'm sceptic; so when I get a piece of information, I measure it against my gut feeling first. If it feels good, I want facts, research and I'll try it on for size, before I make a decision on whether or not this is an all-around good tip. So, I did some research and found a really interesting woman who has a wonderful way to put this all together and made me want to try it out. She's social psychologist Amy Cuddy, and according to her, your body language speaks volumes about you and your emotional predisposition. She goes as far as to say that your body language shapes who you are. Even more interesting than that, you can change your emotional and mental state by changing your posture. Incredible and true! Trust me, I tried this and it works wonders! Although this is great news, it will require some getting used to.

So here's how it works:

When someone lacks confidence they have a tendency to make themselves small. Meaning that they keep their arms close to their bodies with their arms crossed or their hands holding together, they also keep their legs right underneath them or crossed, they're hunched over, etc. This is often unconscious; we take "small" poses when we are in the presence of someone who takes up a lot of space and energy – say, a person of authority or someone who is very dynamic. Taking a "small" pose makes us feel small too, and it heightens cortisol in our system (that's the hormone responsible for stress), so it's not too good for confidence, now is it. On the other hand, someone who is confident will take up more space; put their hands up in the air a few times, or lean one arm over the back of the chair, they'll spread their legs open a little (Oh, come on, don't let your mind go dirty here!) and if they do cross their legs, it'll be ankle over knee, so they still take up some space (please don't do this when wearing a skirt – or at least not in public).

Same thing goes with your tone of voice: if you are self-conscious or lack confidence, your voice will be quieter, have a higher pitch and might even have a tendency to break up. People who have more confidence have a deeper, steadier and stronger voice. There are exceptions to this of course, some people who lack confidence may speak very loudly to be heard and some people who are confidence may speak softly so one can't really base an assumption on that alone. A person's confidence level is harder to detect merely by the sound of their voice, it's much easier to do with body language but I've been studying people for a long time and there's one thing that I have found that hasn't deceived me yet and that is the amount of air that the person lets out, their pauses and the intonation that varies depending on the words they use. Of course I'm not here to give you a course of the matter but I just wanted to slip that interesting piece of information in here so that you know that body language goes beyond your posture. You'll know why this information is pertinent to this section in the exercise that follows. ☺

Ok, let's get back to pure and simple body language.

Here's the fun part: if you take up more space, that is, make yourself "bigger" on purpose, your mind will adjust. Taking up more space will help your levels of testosterone to rise - that's the hormone of power, and yes women have testosterone too.

When I first came across this bit of information I thought it was a little like faking it until you make it, and I really didn't believe it would work. Then I thought: What do I have to lose? Being self-conscious that's what. So I tried the "faking it till you make it" bit with my body language. At first it felt awkward... a lot! So I practiced at home when no one was watching. When it started to feel better, I tried it at work. Instead of making myself small at the conference table, I'd take up just a little more space and moved out from under myself. It took some time before it became comfortable but I immediately started to see a difference in the way I felt and the way people responded around me. I felt calmer, more in control and people responded in a respectful manner, some who were distant, actually started warming up to me.

So if you want to feel more confident, try these simple tricks:

- Hold your head high no matter where you are
- Pull your shoulders back
- Stick your butt out a little (some women have a tendency to tuck their tail bone in)
- Before a meeting, new encounters or a reading in front of the class, go to the nearest bathroom and do the power pose: stand up tall with legs spread a little and arms reaching for the ceiling or on hands on your hips as a power gesture.

Of course if you feel good in your body, this all become easier and the best way to feel good in your body is to eat well and exercise. So we're back to the chapter *Know thyself* of this book. Can you see how everything intertwines? My bet is you are starting to see the big picture. It's not one thing that we do that will level up our confidence; it's all the little things put together.

P.S: To watch a Ted talk video of Amy Cuddy on body language, see the references at the end of this book.

Ok, you've come this far, don't give up now because this next piece is a dozy. Wait for it....

Sensuality is a girl's best friend

« *It isn't what I do, but how I do it. It isn't what I say, but how I say it, and how I look when I do it and say it.* »

- Mae West

Y‍ou read it here gals! We are women and if there's one thing that can't be taken from us is our sensuality. So use it, and use it wisely!

Sensuality has gotten a bad reputation, mainly because of how religions view it as dirty and evil. But it's not! Sensuality is all around us. The dictionary defines it as: "The condition of being pleasing or fulfilling to the senses". Well, I don't know about you but I find nature to be pleasing and fulfilling to the senses, should that be shunned too? Ladies, let's face it. We all want to be fulfilling and pleasing to the senses. Of course we do;

let me tell you something, there is nothing more pleasing to the senses than a woman who is so confident that she dares to be sensual. Actually, I wasn't going to write anything on the subject because I know too little about her but I think this section could use a little Mae West magic. So I would like to invite you to view a great little Youtube video of some of her best moments: https://www.youtube.com/watch?v=FJS67ookmZc

Mae West was way ahead of her time and I'm not suggesting that you should follow in her promiscuous ways but her attitude towards men and life was just so SASSY!! I love it!

Back to our subject: men shouldn't be the only reason why you should make an effort to feel comfortable with your femininity or your sensuality, but if that's where you want to start, than that's fine with me. You have to understand that being sensual doesn't imply that you want to make out with everyone. It's more of a feeling; the feeling of knowing that you *can* be appealing and when you own that, the world is yours.

Does it matter what you are wearing or if you have makeup on? No. Is it a question of boobs or butt? NO! Look, I'm not the sexiest or most beautiful girl out there and I rarely put more than just mascara on my face and I've turned some heads without being "all that". Dressing up and putting make up on, may help you feel better about yourself but it shouldn't take all that. You should feel good about yourself even without make up on or dressing up. That's what confidence is all about.

Sensuality is about owning your feminine side. Sadly, a woman who is not afraid of her femininity, her sensuality, sexuality and ability to enchant is often labelled a slut and even treated as an outcast by other women. In my opinion, though all she's doing is gifting people with her energy. Here is what I'm saying: I find that there isn't much on this planet that is sexier then someone who owns who they are: who aren't afraid to laugh out loud, to smile to a stranger, even to flaunt their good stuff. This is true for women and for men.

Now, don't get me wrong. I'm not saying you should flaunt your stuff just to get your way, that's just being manipulative! But if you are truly yourself, you won't be scared of that sexiness that lives within you and you'll let it shine once in a while.

Here are a few pointers on how to become more sensual:

- Let yourself be drawn to masculine energy. Yes, even if you are in a relationship. I'm not saying go jump the next guy, I'm just saying make note of how you feel in the presence of a man. If you feel nervous or self-conscious, try taking a different pose or smiling.
- When you catch yourself criticizing another woman for being at ease with her feminine side, stop yourself. Think: is it because somewhere deep inside you are jealous of her ease, or her shape? My guess is, if you are really honest with yourself, the answer is probably. So become that which you envy. It's that simple.
- A good way to do that is to surround yourself with women who celebrate their femininity. Hey, if you can't beat them, join them right. * wink.
- Dress in a way that flatters your body and that makes you feel beautiful.
- Smile more
- Learn to walk with more fluidity in your movements; sway your hips and dip your shoulders a little.

   (At Sassy Confidence, we have a "Discover your sensuality" workshop – I got to say, it is so much fun! Join us.)

Bottom line: stop being so prude. I know that's a little harsh, but when you learn to loosen up, you'll worry less and have more fun.

Alright, now I want you to forgive me in advance for this next, not-so-fun part. Beware: I'm gonna be in your face a little... but it's only because I love you ☺ ...

Talking about sensuality without addressing the following issue wouldn't be fair so here we go: women who dress pretty – short skirts or leggings with a nice sexy top then, when they walk down the street and get attention from guys, they flick the finger or send the guy a good old fashion *Fu*.

Look, there is a lot of talk about this topic, these women say: "men shouldn't react like that to women, it's disrespectful." Or "I don't dress like that for them, I do it for me" or "when I get those remarks; its' offensive, I feel violated." Etc. First off, be a real woman and be honest enough with yourself to admit that we don't dress like that for ourselves; we do it to get attention from guys – handsome respectful guys. We only feel violated when we get the attention from a guy that doesn't meet the standard of what we find attractive. So stop being so offended when all the other guys take a look at you; I mean, it's a good thing – it means YOU ARE BEAUTIFUL, they are giving you a compliment for crying out loud, say thank you, not F* off! If you would really be comfortable with your own body and the way you dress, it wouldn't bother you so much if a guy stares or whistles. Most guys who whistle and yell out to you do it to impress their buddies and/or because they are insecure and don't know how to express their attraction to you and emotions in any other way. Let's be honest most men lack creativity in this department. And girls; if you don't like all the attention you are getting; don't dress in such a way to get it.

This being said, I know that there are some real perverts out there and they will take whatever occasion they get to take advantage of women. These men are sick and no matter how you dress they're out to get you. That's just reality and women must deal with that along with everything else. That is why I highly recommend that all women have at the very least one self defense class every year. It gives you confidence and it will give you the tools and techniques that you need to defend yourself, should you ever need it – God forbid! Why every year? Well, just because if you never use a skill it tends to get rusty really fast. One self defense course a year won't kill you, as a matter of fact, it might just save your life. Get a bunch of friends to do it with, have fun! Of course, my other tip, which is just good old common sense, is: don't walk alone in iffy neighborhoods.

*Important note: You should know that men (women too of course) are just like predators; they "smell" uneasiness, insecurity and fear. These emotional states are a sign of weakness. You might as well be walking around with a big sign on your back that says: attack me, I'm weak. Predators will take advantage of that. Don't emanate those emotional states and you'll most probably avoid dealing with their crap. Although it's not normal to *always* feel safe and secure, there are ways to feel safer: seek help if you are an anxious person, have a friend to go places with you, take up a self-defence class, etc.

Have fun!

This might very well be the shortest section of this book but it's one of the best keys you can apply to your everyday life to have your confidence climb up and go through the roof! It stands in these two words: **HAVE FUN!** I swear I can't put enough emphasise on this. Those two words can't be bold enough or big enough!

Life is worth every second. You don't want to come to the end of it and have the 5 regrets of the dying as mentioned in the chapter *Developing greatness.* Because if you look at those really carefully, you'll see they all come down to this: they wish they had more fun. Go back and read them over and you'll see for yourself. When we were children we'd find fun everywhere and in everything. Whatever wasn't fun, we didn't want to do – remember those days? Now, it seems all that is important to us is not fun.

As kids we were carefree and couldn't give a hoot about how we looked or what other people thought. It's amazing how that's attractive, don't you agree? I mean just look at some kids under the age of 7, they are just so natural, and it's so much fun to be around. Where has all the fun gone? We have settled for less and tossed fun aside because of our responsibilities. But when fun goes out the window, so does our happiness, our confidence, our love of life, etc. We slowly let ourselves die through a painfully boring life.

Laughter is said to be the best medicine and when you have no fun there can be no laughter. Go out there and find what is fun again; be silly, watch funny movies, go see a stand-up comic, do something crazy and fun. After all, good memories always have fun as their foundation. Strive to do something fun every day and your confidence will rise again.

As Nike says so well: JUST DO IT!

Confidence in action

Ok girls, this is where things get sweeter. We'll take a look at some areas where confidence in action will get you what you want. Here we go!

Getting the job:

There are many things that you can do to get the job you want, but trust me when I say that if you show little to no confidence during the interview; your chances of getting the job are slim to none. How do I know this? Well for starters, I've worked for over 4 years in as a recruiter in a people placement agency (kind of like head hunting), so you can imagine the amount of interviews I've conducted. Plus, I can say in all honesty that I have never been to an interview and not gotten the job that I applied for, even if I didn't always have the qualifications for it. Nope, I'm not tooting my own horn here, I'm just saying that with these tips, you'll be on your way to getting the job you want!

Alright, so what you want to do is

a) Make sure you can actually do the job you are applying for. I mean, be honest with yourself; don't apply for a job as a nurse if you aren't one, and/or if the job requires you to work nights and you can't handle that, then don't apply for it. Because if you do; first you'll have sucky interview then if you do get the job, you won't be able to do what is required of you properly and efficiently and it will affect your confidence. Don't go there!

b) Dress the part. Don't show up to an interview dressed in slacks like you're going to do work around your house. But don't dress up too much either. If you are going for a job in construction, don't wear a dress to the interview. A nice pair of jeans and a clean shirt would do just fine. An office job, on the other hand, will require a nice pair of dress pants or a dress.

c) Posture. Aside from dressing the part, you don't want to slouch in the chair or look like you are cocky either. Sit up straight, shoulders back. Look at the interviewer in the eye (careful, this is not a stare down contest either), give a good hand shake but don't squish the person's hand.

d) Crank yourself us. There is nothing worst for an employer to sit across from someone that looks like they are about to fall asleep. Listen to some upbeat music beforehand or do the Power Pose as described in the body/mind connexion chapter. Smile during the interview, you want to come across as an enthusiastic person.

e) Participate. Another thing that is very much disliked by bosses are people who give you the shortest possible answer. Try to put some meat around the bone, give more than just a yes or no answer unless it is required. Now, don't stray far and wide and talk for ever either. We want answers, not an entire story line.

f) Honesty. I think I don't need to explain this one, but I will add this: If you don't say upfront what you expect from the job or ask the questions you want the answers too, you're not giving yourself a chance and you aren't being honest with yourself or the potential employer. This screams dissatisfaction, quitting or a burnout waiting to happen.

Always be aware that with any job – even if you are self-employed - there will always people that you don't like or things you don't want to do. There is no avoiding that... other than staying in your living room watching movies all day long for the rest of your life (BORING, and will be the death of your confidence for sure!) Make sure that these dislikes don't weigh too heavy on you. Always respect the 80/20 rule: 80% like of people and job and 20% dislike. Even a 70/30 ratio is good but below that, you'll find it hard to get up in the morning.

General relationships:

Ok, let's start with relationships in general (friends and coworkers) and leave romantic relationships for desert.

First, let me explain something about human relationships, and this applies for the bosses you'll get, the people you deal with, clients, friends, etc. You will attract what you emanate. Meaning, if you lack self-esteem, you might attract a job or friends that take you for granted, that whine a lot, nothing ever goes right in their lives, etc. If you are a go getter, you'll attract people that don't take no for an answer, they've always got some project going or somewhere to be.

There is a saying that goes like this: "Birds of a feather flock together". Basically, what it means is that similar people tend to associate with each other. I use to have a profound aversion to that saying; I use to look around at the friends I had back then and see them criticize everything and nothing ever seemed to go their way in life and I'd think: "My gosh, I'm nothing like that." But now, I know I was. Not necessarily exactly like them but some parts of me were: I didn't criticize out loud but inside, and I didn't do much to change my situation because I thought I didn't have a choice.

Now, listen; if the first expression doesn't speak to you very much as it was for me, here is another one that might be better for you to grasp what I mean – this one from Jim Rhon - it says: "You are the average of the 5 people you spend the most time with." So, think about this and take a good hard look at your friends because they are the reflection of what and who you are. If you don't like what you see, you can do something about it.

You can work on yourself to become a better person and to attract better people. Here is a simple exercise to do just that:

- Think about people that you admire
- Make a list of the things that you admire about them
- Think about the places where these people hang out
- Go hang out there too!

What?! You don't think you can? Why not exactly? Give me one good reason other than the ones that you use to diminish your self-worth.... You can't, can you. Because the only excuses we use are the ones that keep us right where we are; in that rut you think you can't get out of. DARE TO BE BOLDER! The rush is FANTASTIC, and it will get you places and things you want.

Here's a kicker: The qualities that you see in others, you have them too.

It's really simple; you can only see what your mind is capable of accepting. And if your mind is capable of accepting it, then you can do it, you can be it, you can excel at it and you can raise the bar on it. And that's just the way it is.

So the only thing you really need to do, lies within these two steps:

1) Acknowledge that you have these qualities, and
2) Work on amplifying them so they become more noticeable to you and to others.

Long story short; look at the people you hang out with the most; are they spunky, funny, outgoing and confident? Do they tend to be withdrawn intellectuals or gamers? Do they have a life filled with drama – where shit is hitting the fan and people annoy them all week long? Do they act like they are the victims of life? Are they always sick, tired, angry or sad? Be honest with yourself, than love yourself enough to make the necessary changes. If there aren't any changes to be made, then that is absolutely AWESOME, but also highly unlikely! Cause as you already know, no one is perfect and we can all benefit from some form of improvement, and that goes for me too.

Intimate relationships

Ok, desert time!

☺

In my practice I often meet women who really want to be in an intimate relationship but just can't seem to find the right guy (or gal). Again, this is a question of what you emanate: whatever belief lurks in those shadowy corners of your subconscious mind will show up in your life. But there is also a matter of resonance. Let me explain: If you have used drugs before in your life, you might attract someone who is using now or has some kind of dependency be it to love, sex, drugs, etc. This is because that experience you had in the past leaves kind of like a mark or an energy print in your biological energy field. This creates a resonance with others who have the same print in their energy field, much like a beacon of recognition. Hence these people will be attracted to you either because they subconsciously know that you understand them or because they sense somehow that you could help them. Same thing goes for all and any experiences: abuse, neglect, overbearing parents, etc. The resonance goes both ways; you'll find yourself being attracted to that person too.

So, for example; if you lacked confidence somewhere in your life, you will attract someone who has confidence issues too. You will find each other and help each other grow and heal, until you are no longer capable of healing at the same rate. For some this takes years, others lifetimes, others just months.

This being said; to attract someone, you first have to make yourself available. This is not just a matter of being single. It's about having an "I'm looking but I'm not desperate" attitude. The very worst thing that you can do is to feel lonely. What you feel you attract...Remember all those books you probably read on the law of attraction, like *The Secret* by Rhonda Byrne or *The Law of Attraction – the basics of the teachings of Abraham* by Esther and Jerry Hicks... If you haven't read either one, do so! So if you feel lonely and you feel like you can't get the right guy (or gal), guess what; that is exactly what's going to happen. I don't know how many times I've heard people tell me: "I met him (or her) when I stopped looking because I was sure I'd never find anyone." When you stop emanating a feeling of loneliness people will come to you.

Making yourself available also means to put yourself out there, to mingle with likeminded people; take up an activity you'd like to try it will optimize your chances of meeting someone. PS: yoga might not be the place to go, not too many guys there... Unless, of course, you are looking for a gal then, by all means, go do yoga – If yoga, is your sort of thing. ☺

*Side note: from here on, I'll be writing as if the partner you are looking for is a guy. If it's not, please don't be offended. It's just easier to write this way and know that the same principles apply to women looking for women.

Ok, let's be honest, us girls we think we know what guys looks for... but I've hung out with a lot of men and let me tell ya, some will surprise the hell out of you! So I did a little investigation; I asked a bunch of men from ages 20 to 65, to be brutally honest about what they find attractive in a woman... that is if they were to spend more than a one night stand with her. Now, this is not a scientific research or anything but it sure gives a pretty good over view.

Now, when you look at this chart you have to remember that this has been taken from just a small collection of men, but in this "teaser", you can already see that men don't just look for the perfect Barbie figure that we all think they do. Of course they find women who are well proportioned appealing to their senses, but then again, if you are completely honest with yourself as a woman, you probably find that well-proportioned women look good too, otherwise you wouldn't get upset when your man stares at one By the way, that's called jealousy, and it is a nasty little thing that you should get rid of! Thankfully, when using the tips in this book; you will raise your confidence levels and become less and less jealous of others because you'll realize that you can have it all too if you really put yourself into it.

Ok so back to those stats. Here they are:

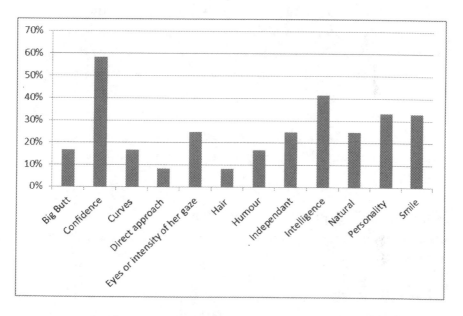

As the chart clearly demonstrates; confidence, intelligence and personality all rank much higher and the "appealing scale" then any body part. Of course, not everything ended up on this chart because it would have taken up too much space and/or wasn't fit for the point I wanted to make, for instance; actual height and weight, or hair color and length, and even the level of education (yes, there's a difference between education and intelligence). All this was to prove one point and one point only: there isn't one particular look, size, weight or color that you need to be in order to attract the guy that is going to be right for you.

So how do you attract that guy?

Well, for starters, I'm pretty sure he won't appear out of thin air in your living room unless you have some kind of genie lamp I don't know of, so you have to get up, make yourself pretty and go out. Do you need to go to a night club? Nope! You can meet a guy wherever you want to hang out: golf, tennis, at work, in the library, paintball, through friends of friends, gym, etc. There is no wrong place to meet "the one". Now, there are some places where you may be more likely to pick up a one night stand (ie: bar or gym), than anywhere else but if you've learned how to use your intuition and some good old common sense, that won't happen… unless you want it too. Look you probably heard someone say that the worst place to meet a guy is in a club, well you know what, I met my husband at the bar where I use to work 19 years ago, and some of my friends have met in the same way. So maybe the people that started that rumor just weren't lucky.

Moving on… if a guy catches your eye, don't play too shy. Show interest: smile, toss your hair back, and move closer to him if he doesn't approach you first.

Let me tell you about a really interesting research that was done on how men and women react to one another during the initial meeting. This research was aired on Channel 4 in the UK and is available on Youtube (see References for link). In this documentary, researchers have discovered that it's not men, but women who initiate things. They go about saying that courtship is almost always a matter of female choice. (See I told you we had power *wink!) The woman will "tell" a man that she is interested and that he can approach her by sending him a tell tail sign (hopefully the guy picks up on it), usually, this is a luxurious smile in his direction. Please, take some time to view the above mentioned video, it will give you great advice on dating approaches; the signs you emit and those of others. Trust me; it doesn't get much better than that!

Look as with anything in life, you shouldn't settle until you find what's right for you, this includes "the guy". He must like you just the way you are, encourage you when you have a project, pick you up when you're down, make you smile and help around the house ☺. No but seriously, before you go out there to look for mister perfect, make sure you are clear of what you are looking for. Your list should look a little like this (note this is what I like. What you like may be like this or totally different and that's OK – these are just examples):

Must have:	Avoid at all cost:	Tolerable:
• He has and is able to keep a good job • He is supportive of my projects • He is confident and trusting • Must be equal height or taller than me • Be active • Humour	• Jealous type • Guy with too much of a big ego • Clingy / emotionally dependant • Who has drug, alcohol or game dependence	• Age difference • Has a hobby that takes a lot of time (so long as he makes time for us and responsibilities) • Smoking –as long as he respect me and not smoke in house or in car.

The reason for the three columns is because you have to know that there is <u>no such thing as the perfect guy</u>. Every guy you'll meet will have his flaws – as do you. There are some things that you'll be able to tolerate, others you won't, and things you absolutely need in order to be in a fulfilling intimate relationship. You have to know these things before you start looking. But also, give a guy the chance to prove to you that he can be the one. Don't drop him like and old rag just because he combed his hair wrong (unless that's one of the things you just can't stand, in which case I highly suggest you revise your values. But I know you're not like that☺).

Wrapping it up

I'm sure you've noticed that I mention honesty a few times in this book. The reason for this is that you can't expect to have good strong confidence if you are constantly lying to yourself or to others. Lies end up being hard to keep up with and they are the absolute worst thing for your self-esteem and your confidence – let's not even mention they are relationship killers. Plus as I always say: Honesty is power because it makes room for you to create lasting and desirable change. So be powerful - be honest!

To finish this book, I want to share one last principle that I live by and so does Anthony Robins and this is how it goes:

See things as they are, not worse than they are.

I'm big on positive thinking but if you go to a garden and chant affirmations all day long in hopes to get the weeds out. What do you think will happen? Nothing! Open your eyes, see the weeds, bend over and pluck them out! This is a metaphor of course but you get the picture; if something isn't working for you, pluck it out of your life. Make the decision and take action – no matter what others say. After all, it's your life, not theirs!

This being said, you will find many naysayers on your journey to your very own sassy confidence. They will tell you that it's all nonsense; that you can go through life fairly well without all of what you learned in this little book, and you know what, they are right.... But is this what you want; to go through life "fairly well"? I surely don't! I want to go through life walking my own path, plant all the good things I want in it and take what I don't want out. I am the designer! I want to set the stones I'll walk on, I want to walk in a room and hear people say "Wow, I'd like to be fearless like that", not because it flatters my ego but because I know that when that happens, I'm in the position to make a difference in someone's life, or even in this world, I want to lead by my example. I have kids... Well, they are teens now, soon to be young adults, and this is what I want for them and for you. I want you to look back at your life and say: "Yep, that's pretty darn good. I'm good with that." Instead of having regrets about things you could have done or what you could have been.

It all starts with you! And that's why I created Sassy Confidence. I hope I've given you the gentle push and the tools you need to build that confidence that is already within you! Don't forget that confidence isn't built overnight, so I suggest you keep a confidence journal and jot down something every single day that made you feel confident. When you lack confidence, take a look at those entries in your journal and do what it takes to feel better.

If I only had one thing to wish for is that you see that you have to power to become what you've always wanted to be, after all, you hold it all within. You just need to dust it off a little. I hope you don't limit yourself and don't let anyone limit you either.

Well, now that you've got all this information, it's time... It's time for you to go out there and shine!

Hey, I'm the kind of girl that likes to connect with people; I'd like to hear from you. Join us www.fb.com/sassyconfidence and share your story. What did you do to raise your confidence levels? Can't wait to hear from you!

About the author

The first thing you need to know is that I don't take myself seriously, I love to kid around and have fun because I believe that life should be fun, always! But I do have a "messenger/teacher" side to me. I also believe that although life should be fun, you should learn stuff to better yourself every single day, until your last. I guess what I'm saying is: have the curiosity of a child, be always ready to learn something new and apply it to your life – if it fits your values of course. Well, in a nut shell, that explains why I've studied so many different things and why I always have projects on the roll.

I have studied Feminine Divine spirituality and have a master's in the art of Metaphysics. I'm also a hypnotherapist... and that's just the short version of the list.

I have made it my life's work to help women and kids to have better confidence and self-esteem. In that sense, I have worked with the Cadets and Junior Canadian Rangers, and also participated in a writing board to renew the program on the broad subjects of positive youth development and adolescent development. I also work in collaboration with Dove® giving workshops on self-esteem and body image for girls and of course, as you now know, I give workshops for women's confidence all over.

The combination of my personal experience, my research and my studies has cumulated in the founding of the Sassy Confidence movement. But I've also created www.easy4ubusiness.com to give women the tools they need to make money from their passion and creative forces. I truly believe that women can change the world with their genuine kindness and inner strengths. Now a day, it's even easier than ever before because the world is at our fingertip, that's why I also specialise in Social Media Marketing and management – to reach more people and change more lives!

Join us at www.fb.com/sassyconfidence (we don't bite, I swear!) there is a bunch of cool info, quotes and all our events are listed there. Come share your story with us!

You can even create your own event, invite some friends, we'll make a cool afternoon (or evening) out of it; I'd love to meet you!

Never forget; "*that woman*" you want to be; she wants
to come out too, so don't hold her back – have fun with
it! SHINE with all your Sassy Confidence!

References

❖ **Sassy Confidence** :
  ➢ On Facebook: www.fb.com/sassyconfidence
  ➢ On Pinterest : http://www.pinterest.com/sassyconfidence/
  ➢ On Tumblr : http://sassyconfidence.tumblr.com/
  ➢ On Twitter : https://twitter.com/Sassyconfidenc1

❖ **Easy 4u Business** : www.easy4ubusiness.com

❖ **Article on the power in a drop of water**:
  http://media.cns-snc.ca/history/waterdrop/waterdrop.html

❖ **Body language:**
  ➢ Watch a fun 21 minutes Ted talk video with Amy cuddy. In this video she explains how body language shapes who we are.
  http://www.ted.com/talks/amy_cuddy_your_body_language_shapes_who_you_are?language=en

❖ **Youtube Video of Mae West:**
  https://www.youtube.com/watch?v=FJS670okmZc

❖ **Channel 4 UK documentary: Body language, indicators of interest:**
  https://www.youtube.com/watch?v=SBOtj1RmaUE